THE FOREST OF FEAR

Written by Catherine Baker

Illustrated by Tom Percival

Rocket and I travelled for many days.

At last we reached the wild forest.

It was spooky and quiet.

"We need to find a scorched twig, Rocket," I said.

"We must take it back to the Grand Master. Help me look!"

Suddenly, Rocket barked.

He shot out of sight.

I could see a red light gleaming
in the sky. I ran to find Rocket.

Flames were creeping right up
to him.

"We must put the flames out,
Rocket!" I cried.

q

Rocket found a stream nearby.

I reached for the box in my backpack.

Inside the box was a foot pump!

It took a long time to fight the flames.
At last the forest was safe.

Rocket spotted a scorched twig, lying right next to a bag.

Inside the bag were two padded jackets ... and a map!